The Six Stages of Building Wealth

A Comprehensive Guide to Financial Independence

Patrick Odega

Dedication

This section of the book is dedicated to all the individuals who have embarked on the journey of building wealth. To those who have struggled, persisted, and succeeded in achieving financial independence, this book is dedicated to you. You are an inspiration to others who aspire to achieve their own financial goals. May the knowledge and strategies outlined in this book help you continue to grow your wealth and live the life of your dreams.

Contents

Acknowledgments

I would like to express my sincere gratitude to all those who have contributed to the creation of this book on the six stages of building wealth.

Firstly, I would like to thank all the financial experts and authors whose works have inspired and informed my own writing. Your research, insights, and expertise have been instrumental in shaping the ideas and strategies presented in this book.

I would also like to thank my editor, who provided invaluable feedback and guidance throughout the writing and editing process. Their attention to detail and editorial expertise helped to refine this book into its final form.

I would like to express my appreciation to all the readers who have chosen to invest their time and attention in this book. I hope that the insights and strategies presented in these pages will be of value to you as you pursue your own path toward financial independence.

Finally, I would like to thank my family and friends for their unwavering support and encouragement throughout the writing process. Your love and encouragement have been a constant source of inspiration, and I am grateful for your presence in my life.

Introduction

The desire for financial independence is a universal aspiration. We all want to be in control of our financial future and enjoy the freedom and security that wealth can provide. However, building wealth can be a daunting and challenging task, requiring dedication, discipline, and a solid plan of action.

This book is designed to provide a clear and concise roadmap for building wealth in six stages. Each stage is focused on different strategies and tactics that can help readers achieve their financial goals, whether they are just starting out on their wealth-building journey or looking to take their wealth to the next level.

The first chapter focuses on building a strong foundation, including creating a budget, establishing an emergency fund, paying off debt, and building credit. Chapter two covers saving and investing, including setting financial goals, creating a savings plan, and investing in stocks, bonds, and other assets. Chapter three explores creating passive income streams, such as rental property investing, dividend investing, and creating an online business.

Chapter four delves into building a business, including entrepreneurship, marketing and sales, and creating a sustainable source of income. Chapter five discusses protecting wealth through insurance, estate planning, asset protection, and safeguarding your wealth for future generations. Lastly, chapter six covers giving back through philanthropy, charitable giving, community service, and using wealth to make a positive impact on the world.

In the following chapters, we will delve into each stage in greater detail, providing practical advice and strategies for building wealth and achieving financial independence. Whether you are just starting out on your journey or looking to accelerate your progress, the insights and strategies presented in these pages can help you reach your financial goals and enjoy the life of your dreams.

he Desire for Financial Independence:

At the heart of building wealth is the desire for financial independence. This means having the resources and freedom to live the life you want, without being limited by financial constraints. Financial independence allows you to pursue your passions, take risks, and enjoy the fruits of your labor.

However, achieving financial independence requires discipline and sacrifice. It requires making smart financial decisions, avoiding debt, and investing in assets that appreciate in value over time. It also means being willing to delay gratification and resist the temptation to overspend or make impulsive financial decisions.

The Challenges of Building Wealth:

Building wealth is not easy, and there are many challenges along the way. The biggest challenge for many people is simply getting started. It can be overwhelming to think about all the steps required to build wealth, and it can be hard to know where to begin.

Another challenge is staying motivated and disciplined over the long term. Building wealth is a marathon, not a sprint, and it requires sustained effort and dedication over many years. It can be easy to get discouraged or distracted along the way, particularly when faced with setbacks or unexpected expenses.

Finally, building wealth requires a certain degree of financial literacy and knowledge. It is important to understand the basics of personal finance, including budgeting, saving, investing, and managing debt. Without this knowledge, it can be difficult to make informed financial decisions and achieve long-term financial success.

The Six Stages of Building Wealth:

Despite the challenges, building wealth is possible for anyone who is willing to put in the effort and follow a clear plan of action. The six stages of building wealth presented in this book provide a roadmap for achieving financial independence and living the life you want.

Each stage builds on the previous one, and together they create a comprehensive framework for building wealth over the long term. By following the strategies and tactics presented in each chapter, readers can take control of their finances, build wealth, and achieve financial independence.

Chapter 1:

Building a Strong Foundation

Building a strong foundation is the first stage of building wealth. It involves establishing good financial habits and practices that set the stage for long-term success. The following are the key components of building a strong foundation:

Creating a Budget:

Creating a budget is the first step in taking control of your finances. It involves tracking your income and expenses and identifying areas where you can cut back and save money. By creating a budget, you can ensure that you are living within your means and saving for your financial goals.

Establishing an Emergency Fund:

Establishing an emergency fund is an important part of building a strong financial foundation. It involves setting aside a portion of your income to cover unexpected expenses, such as car repairs, medical bills, or job loss. By having an emergency fund, you can avoid going into debt and protect your long-term financial goals.

Paying off Debt:

Paying off debt is an essential part of building a strong financial foundation. It involves prioritizing high-interest debt, such as credit card debt, and paying it off as quickly as possible. By paying off debt, you can reduce your monthly expenses and free up money for other financial goals, such as saving and investing.

Building Credit:

Building good credit is an important part of building a strong financial foundation. It involves using credit responsibly and making timely payments on loans and credit cards. By building good credit, you can qualify for lower interest rates on loans and credit cards, which can save you money over the long term.

Overall, building a strong foundation is essential for achieving long-term financial success. By creating a budget, establishing an emergency fund, paying off debt, and building good credit, you can set the stage for achieving your financial goals and building wealth over time.

Chapter 2:

Saving and Investing

Saving and investing are critical components of building wealth. Here's a more detailed explanation of the topics you mentioned:

Setting Financial Goals:

The first step in saving and investing is to set financial goals. This involves determining what you want to achieve with your money and how much you'll need to save to reach those goals. Common financial goals include retirement, buying a house, paying for a child's education, and building an emergency fund.

Creating a Savings Plan:

Once you've set your financial goals, the next step is to create a savings plan. This involves identifying how much you need to save each month to reach your goals, as well as deciding where to save your money. For short-term goals, such as a down payment on a house, you might consider a savings account. For long-term goals, such as retirement, you might consider a 401(k), IRA, or other investment account.

Investing in Stocks, Bonds, and Other Assets:

Investing involves putting your money to work to generate long-term growth and income. Some common types of investments include stocks, bonds, mutual funds, and real estate. Each type of investment has its own risks and rewards, and it's important to diversify your portfolio to reduce risk.

When investing in stocks, you can purchase shares of individual companies or invest in mutual funds or exchange-traded funds (ETFs), which provide exposure to a broad range of stocks. When investing in bonds, you can purchase individual bonds or invest in bond funds. Real estate investments can include rental properties, real estate investment trusts (REITs), or crowdfunding platforms.

Making Your Money Work for You:

The final step in saving and investing is to make your money work for you. This means maximizing the return on your investments and minimizing fees and taxes. To do this, you should regularly review your investment portfolio and make adjustments as needed. You should also consider working with a financial advisor who can help you create a personalized investment plan and provide guidance on investment decisions.

Saving and investing are essential for building wealth. By setting financial goals, creating a savings plan, investing in a diversified portfolio of assets, and making your money work for you, you can achieve your long-term financial goals and build wealth over time.

It's worth noting that saving and investing are not mutually exclusive strategies. In fact, the most successful investors often have a savings plan in place as well. This is because saving provides a financial cushion that can help protect your investments in times of market volatility or economic uncertainty.

When creating a savings plan, it's important to consider your personal financial situation and goals. This may include factors such as your income, expenses, debt, and risk tolerance. By understanding these factors, you can create a savings plan that is tailored to your individual needs and circumstances.

Investing in a diversified portfolio of assets can also help mitigate risk and increase the likelihood of long-term growth. A diversified portfolio typically includes a mix of stocks, bonds, and other assets that are spread across different industries, sectors, and regions. This can help protect your investments against market fluctuations and economic downturns.

Making your money work for you involves taking steps to maximize your returns and minimize fees and taxes. This may include regularly reviewing your investment portfolio, rebalancing your assets as needed, and seeking out low-cost investment options. It's also important to consider the impact of taxes on your investments, and to work with a financial advisor or tax professional to optimize your tax strategy.

Ultimately, saving and investing are key components of building wealth, but they are just one part of a larger financial plan. Other important considerations include managing debt, building credit, and protecting your assets with insurance. By taking a comprehensive approach to your finances and working towards your long-term financial goals, you can achieve financial independence and build a better future for yourself and your family.

Chapter 3:

Creating Passive Income Streams

Creating passive income streams is an important part of building long-term wealth. Unlike active income, which requires ongoing work and effort, passive income allows you to earn money without having to constantly trade your time and energy.

There are several ways to create passive income streams, including rental property investing, dividend investing, creating an online business, and generating income without trading time for money.

Rental property investing involves purchasing and renting out properties, such as apartments, houses, or commercial buildings. This can provide a steady stream of rental income that can be reinvested or used to cover expenses. However, it's important to carefully consider the costs and risks associated with owning and managing rental properties, including maintenance, repairs, and vacancies.

Dividend investing involves investing in stocks or funds that pay regular dividends. Dividends are payments made by a company to its shareholders, typically as a portion of profits. This can provide a steady stream of passive income that can be reinvested or used to cover expenses.

Creating an online business can also be a great way to generate passive income. This may include creating and selling digital products, such as e-books, courses, or software, or monetizing a blog or website through advertising or affiliate marketing. However, building a successful online business takes time and effort, and it's important to have a clear business plan and marketing strategy in place.

Generating income without trading time for money may involve creating a product or system that can be sold repeatedly, such as an e-book or an online course. This allows you to earn money without having to constantly create new products or services. Alternatively, you may be able to generate passive income through investments, such as real estate or stocks, that appreciate in value over time.

Creating passive income streams is a key component of building wealth and achieving financial independence. By diversifying your income sources and finding ways to earn money without trading time for money, you can create a more stable and secure financial future.

However, it's important to keep in mind that creating passive income streams often requires a significant amount of upfront work and investment. It's not a quick fix for financial struggles or a substitute for hard work and dedication.

Moreover, it's essential to research and understand the risks and potential rewards associated with each passive income strategy before investing your time and money. Additionally, it's important to have a solid understanding of personal finance, including budgeting, investing, and risk management, before embarking on any passive income venture.

In summary, creating passive income streams is an excellent way to build long-term wealth and achieve financial independence. It allows you to diversify your income sources, reduce your reliance on active income, and create a more stable and secure financial future. However, it's important to approach passive income strategies with caution, do your due diligence, and be prepared to put in the necessary work and investment to see long-term success.

Chapter 4:

Building a Business

Building a successful business is another key stage of building wealth. Entrepreneurs who are willing to take calculated risks and are passionate about their ideas can create a sustainable source of income that can provide financial freedom and independence.

One of the first steps to building a business is identifying a problem in the market and developing a unique solution that can address it. This involves conducting market research, identifying your target audience, and understanding their needs and pain points.

Once you have a solid business idea, the next step is developing a marketing and sales strategy that can effectively reach your target audience and drive sales. This can involve building a website, developing a social media presence, creating marketing materials, and networking with potential customers and partners.

To build a sustainable source of income, it's essential to focus on creating a strong foundation for your business. This includes developing efficient processes, building a strong team, and creating a culture of innovation and continuous improvement. Additionally, it's important to develop a long-term growth strategy that can scale your business and ensure its long-term success.

However, building a successful business also requires dedication, hard work, and a willingness to take risks. It's important to have a clear understanding of your goals, develop a realistic business plan, and seek advice and support from mentors and other successful entrepreneurs.

It's also important to understand that building a successful business takes time and may involve setbacks and challenges along the way. It's essential to remain focused, persistent, and flexible in your approach, continually learning and adapting as you go.

In addition, building a successful business also offers the opportunity to create value for others and have a positive impact on the world. By developing products or services that solve real-world problems and contribute to society, you can create a business that has a meaningful and lasting impact.

Finally, building a successful business also requires a commitment to ethical and sustainable practices. By prioritizing social responsibility and environmental sustainability, you can build a business that not only generates wealth but also contributes to a better world for future generations.

Overall, building a successful business is a challenging but rewarding stage of building wealth. By taking calculated risks, being passionate and innovative, and committing to ethical and sustainable practices, you can create a business that provides financial rewards, personal fulfillment, and a positive impact on the world.

Chapter 5:

Protecting Wealth

Protecting your wealth is an important stage of building wealth, and it involves taking steps to safeguard your assets and investments. This stage includes various strategies that can help you protect your wealth, such as insurance, estate planning, asset protection, and safeguarding your wealth for future generations.

Insurance is a critical tool for protecting your wealth, and it includes various types of insurance such as life insurance, health insurance, disability insurance, and property and casualty insurance. By having adequate insurance coverage, you can protect yourself and your family from unexpected events that can cause financial hardship.

Estate planning is another essential component of protecting your wealth, and it involves creating a plan for distributing your assets and property after your death. This includes creating a will, establishing trusts, and designating beneficiaries for retirement accounts and life insurance policies.

Asset protection is also crucial for safeguarding your wealth, and it involves taking steps to protect your assets from lawsuits, creditors, and other potential threats. This includes strategies such as forming a limited liability company (LLC), creating a trust, and setting up offshore accounts.

Finally, safeguarding your wealth for future generations is an important consideration for those who want to pass their wealth down to their children and grandchildren. This includes establishing a family trust, creating a succession plan, and setting up a charitable foundation or trust to support causes that are important to you.

Overall, protecting your wealth is a crucial stage of building wealth, and it involves taking proactive steps to safeguard your assets and investments. By implementing strategies such as insurance, estate planning, asset protection, and safeguarding your wealth for future generations, you can protect your financial well-being and leave a lasting legacy for your family and the causes you care about.

Chapter 6:

Giving Back

Giving back is an important stage of building wealth that involves using your resources to make a positive impact on the world. As you accumulate wealth, it's important to consider the impact you can have on your community and the world at large.

Philanthropy is one way to give back, and it involves donating money, time, or resources to support causes you care about. Charitable giving is another way to give back and involves donating money to charitable organizations to support their mission and programs. Additionally, community service provides an opportunity to give back by volunteering your time and skills to support local initiatives and organizations.

Using your wealth to make a positive impact on the world can bring a sense of purpose and fulfillment, while also creating a lasting legacy for generations to come. By supporting causes that align with your values and passions, you can create positive change and make a meaningful difference in the world.

It's important to note that giving back doesn't have to wait until you've accumulated significant wealth. Even small acts of kindness and charity can make a difference in someone's life and contribute to a more positive world.

In fact, incorporating giving back into your wealth-building plan from the beginning can provide a sense of purpose and fulfillment throughout the journey. It can also inspire others to do the same, creating a ripple effect of positive change in the world.

Overall, giving back is an important stage of building wealth that should not be overlooked. By incorporating philanthropy, charitable giving, community service, and using your wealth to make a positive impact, you can create a more fulfilling and purpose-driven life while also leaving a lasting legacy for generations to come.

Conclusion

In conclusion, building wealth is an essential part of achieving financial independence and creating a fulfilling life. By following the six stages outlined in this book - building a strong foundation, saving and investing, creating passive income streams, building a business, protecting wealth, and giving back - you can create a solid roadmap for achieving your financial goals.

Throughout the journey, it's important to stay focused, disciplined, and persistent in your efforts. It may not always be easy, but the rewards of building wealth and achieving financial independence can be significant, both for yourself and for those around you.

In summary, the six stages of building wealth are interconnected, and each stage builds upon the previous one. By setting clear financial goals, creating a plan, and taking action, you can move closer to achieving financial freedom and living the life you've always dreamed of.

www.ingramcontent.com/pod-product-compliance
Lightning Source LLC
Chambersburg PA
CBHW070907220526
45466CB00005B/2165